ALSO BY DAVID MELTZER

POETRY

Ragas (1959)
The Clown (1960)
The Process (1965)
The Dark Continent (1967)
Round the Poem Box (1969)
Yesod (1969)
From Eden Book (1969)
Greenspeech (1970)
Luna (1970)
Knots (1971)
Bark (1973)
Tens, Selected Poems: 1961-71 (1973)
Hero/Lil (1973)
The Eyes, the Blood (1973)
Blue Rags (1974)
Harps (1975)

PROSE

*We All Have Something to Say to Each Other:
   An Essay on Kenneth Patchen* (1962)
Bazascope Mother (1964)
Journal of the Birth (1967)
The Agency Trilogy (1968-9)
Orf (1969)
The Martyr (1969)
Brain-Plant Tetralogy (1969-70)
Star (1970)
The San Francisco Poets (1971)
Birth (1973)

TRANSLATION

Morning Glories by Shiga Naoya (in collaboration with
   Allen Say) (1976)

ANTHOLOGIES

The Secret Garden: Anthology of the Classical Kabbalah
   (1976)
Golden Gate: Interviews with Five San Francisco Poets
   (1976)

David Meltzer
SIX

SANTA BARBARA
BLACK SPARROW PRESS
1976

SIX. Copyright © 1976 by David Meltzer.

All rights reserved. Printed in the United States of America. No part of this book may be used or reproduced in any manner whatsoever without written permission except in the case of brief quotations embodied in critical articles and reviews. For information address Black Sparrow Press, P.O. Box 3993, Santa Barbara, CA. 93105.

ACKNOWLEDGEMENTS

Earlier versions of "Vav", "Tree", and "Lights" appeared in *Isthmus*; "Cracks" appeared in an early version in *Tree: 4*; portions of "Apple" appeared in *The Holy Beggars' Gazette* and *Tree 5*; "Face" appeared in *Stations 3 & 4*.

LIBRARY OF CONGRESS CATALOGING IN PUBLICATION DATA

Meltzer, David.
    Six.

    I. Title.
PS3563.E45S5   811'.5'4   76-40038
ISBN 0-87685-271-1
ISBN 0-87685-270-3 pbk.

This book is offered to the memory of
Wallace Berman whose work and presence
brought me face to face with the Aleph.

TABLE OF CONTENTS

Vav	9
Face	33
Tree	55
Lights	61
Cracks	77
Apple	95
Post-Carte	125

VAV

1.

How I follow the angel out of me.
A line of light in photographs of freeways at night.
Picasso draws on space with a flashlight.
The angel shapes itself.

Wind-rose. Neon star. Spire.
Bordered by gold turrets.
Rabbi beards bend down to kiss a book.
Miles of meander sewn into each carpet page unrolled.
Each curl a snake writing through topsoil.
Each letter a song turning into a river.
Follow his lights.

Constant reshaping.
New passage. Ways.
Exit. Entry.
So many signs left to discover.

Light chorus.
Cross-currents.
Get me squinting in a booth.

Whoever speaks works sparks.
Blinking seeds. Lion eyes.

2.

Take me with you, asks the angel.
I have no place no name nothing.
I am Angel of the Void. Vav.
Laughed out of Sky Academy.
I have no shadow.
My wings fold inward as in a tulip bulb.
I am the flower contained. Held back.
Free me.

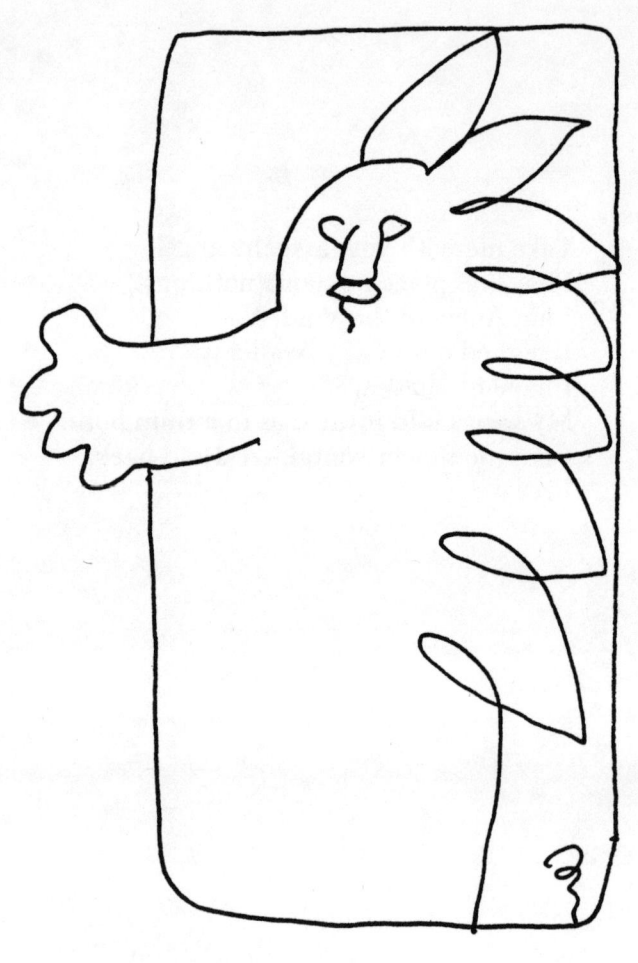

3.

Vav circles me.
Zero the letter.
Bend to a dance of broken mazda.

Open thy sty.
Honey pus-drops stream down thy mask.

Void Angel Vav.
Flea in my heart.
Pain of acquainting.
Are we not man & wife.
Brother & sister.

The page no place for such songs.

Shimmer a whisper of flesh.
Bones are milk.
Body a breath.

Yod Void Angel Vav.
Diamonds on trees in morning.
Linger for praise.
Melach a hymn before sunrays.
Burn out the glitter.

4.

The first day.
Angel shadows mean nothing to rivers.
Frog speck sperming in mud.
Gas plasm belching out of mountains.

The first day.
Natal strings. Monkey ribbons.
Confetti. Porridge.
Shape makes itself up from the soup.

The first Daleth is the first man's longing.
Circumcised. Straight out. At attention.
Vibrating.

The first Daleth stands on one leg.
Bottom jaw of skull.
Stonehenge hangs by a thread.

Daleth. Fool of man's first longing.
The first day.
Holds back nothing.
Nobody is ever surprised again.

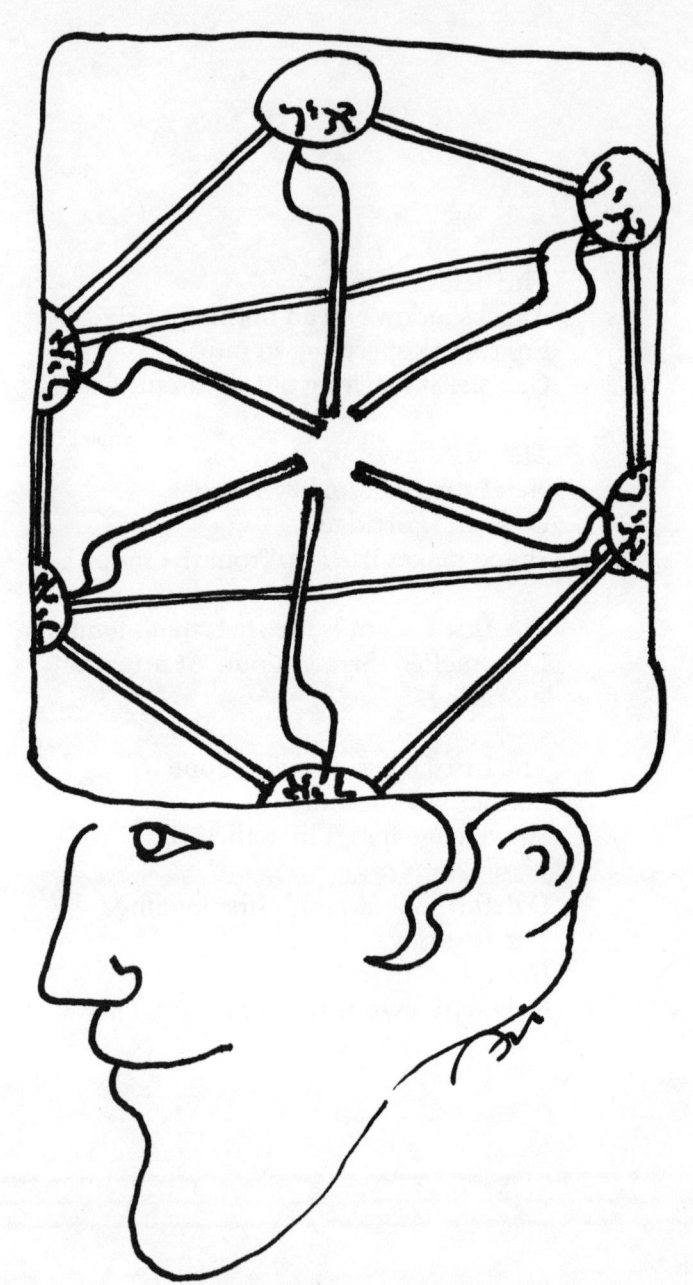

5.

The Angel said it was everywhere.
A despair.
Shadow snuffers.
Spark suckers.
Rob screens with vacuum cleaners.
Power the quest that ends us.
Piled-up dirt & broken stairs.
Golems empty of angels.
Swords upraised. War movies.
Our blood. Spreads into hasidic hair.
The shawl is on fire.

Innerlute

Right now the Angel dictates song.
Snatches my gullibles. Gutteral alarms.

I sing on a home-made tinfoil stage.
Spit seed into space.
Spray rows one, two & three.
Others want their dough back.
Grey eyed jackals.
Hide cassette thumbprints of my song.
Beneath their tongues.

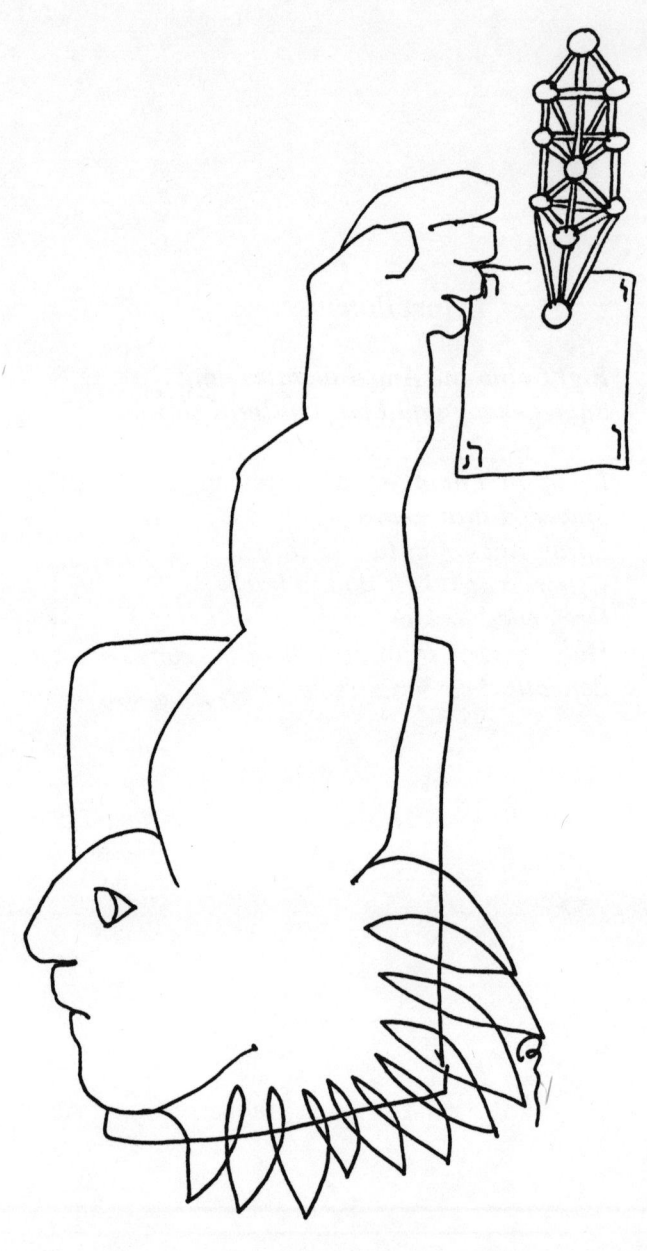

6.

The Angel breaks down.
His light cant bend around.
Thick lead walls surround.
Grail & Aleph alike.

A sniper snapshots wails.
Facts pass into shadow into memory.
Yesterday's news.
I sing through my Angel.

Nobody sees her wings.

7.

Squat to deliver the Angel.
Push.
Oceans overtake the cup you balance on.
Each move forever essential.
The Angel rides free of all spectators.

We return to a pipe.
Sunlight taps our heads.
Sit on the back porch
Marvel at flying ibis.
Pinetop to pinetop.

8.

Angel wont be invoked.
Ancient folios are not Yellow Pages.

One appropriate angel.
Appears in the center of a star.
In the center of a circle.
In the center of a name.

Vav whispers:
Diagrams, wheels, letters, stars.
Decor.
Keep the eye distracted from the visible.
Let a fool unwind his navel.
Soon the cord will end.

9.

Who is the angel with a beard of books.
Shelled like a pea.
Row of angel embryos up & down his spine.

10.

The kid asks.
Did the angel who came out deliver itself like a baby.
Or was it a rose my mouth spoke into your life.

[1972]

FACE

About face.
How to begin.
To make a face begin.
How.
From top to bottom
Or chin to dome?

They say he cant,
You cant,
Face it.
Face the music.
They say you cant face it.
That music between you.
She hears nothing but music.

Words attack face like lice.
Attach to paper.
Music in circles.
She hears nothing but music.

Each eyebrow a seismograph.
En face.
Greek in her left eye.
Hebrew in the right.

I saw her yesterday.
In furs.
Grey streaked red with fox.
In a room playing Chinese checkers.
Very chic.
Art collects itself.
Look her up & down.
She leaves nothing behind.

She hears nothing but music.
Last night she was a fire.
Burning all the books.
Forests fold together like hands.
Words in each tree unpeel.
Race through the world.
Silk. I reach too late.
Incense of her shadow.
It isnt done with words.
She hears only the music.
It is faceless.
I am not there.
Music is all she hears.

All from a place we can not face.

Snapshot. Cartoon. Memory.
Places shape face.
Faces cut away from faces.
Words broken into words.

Age of faces pass by.
Epigrams. Poems.
Emblems with eyes.
Pass by.

Face memory with a wall.
Seal it up.
It'll be years before she escapes.
Into fiction. A Poe finale.
Lovecraft.
Scratchy acetate of ancient radio.

What is told is not what faces you.
What returns has no face.

Face the other.
Faceless passion.
Behind glass.
Fingers tear at it.
Face the other.
Faceless one.
Gone when eyes open.

Face the wall.
Forehead to stone.
Bricks scrape thought.
All is possible.
Bullets spring the river.

Face the wall.
Hands tied.
Pressed against.
Base of spine.

No cigarette.
No match.
No rites.
Crow squawks.
Up there.
Free.
I hear it.

All the points make a face.
Face a mask.
Parzuf.
Dark alleyways.
Office passageways.
Out of synch.
Run out.
Onto carnivale boardwalk.
Into haunted house.
Pounce.
Ghost feathers.
Insistent mechanical laughter.
Radium eyes.
Instep needles.
Trapdoor.
Chute into ocean.

Face the seeker sees as his.
In art.
In air.
In night sky. Black fire.
Stars compose it.

Mirth. A river of faces.
Capped with smiles.
Teeth foam.
All for a camera.
All for my vision.
All in wheels.
Up & down my spine.
Lines I write & fish with.

Face legions.
Stream by. Pop open.
Within eye, face.
Jess roses.
Womb roses.
Ancient scanners of the body.
Passing through.
Adjust goggle.
Erase slain fool of words.

"I can't face it,"
The other voice says.
Immediately.
After head-on collision.

"Face it or fake it,"
Another one says.
Instantly.
Three 38 slugs re-shape reality.

"Face it or forget it."
Turning newspaper pages.

Your face is all the other faces.

Catch my face on mirrors of eyes.

I can not face the nation.
Its broken face.
Nothing left.
Postcard skull & bones.
Brittle as papyrus.
Speech shadows move by.
Fists & pitchforks.
Assassins surround & devour the core.

Medea the mamma.
Draws bloody babes against breasts.
Milked into flags.
Bandages around her abdomen.
No more babies.

This is a recording.

Erzulie.
Tongues point into you.
Knives.
Your space.
Star marked.
Acts of exchange.
Wound, my song.
You are my tongue.
O Shekinah.
Matronita.
Bessie Smith.
Erzulie.
White chickenfeathers.
Snowflakes.
Pour from your red mouth.
White mixed with red.
Black afternoon.
Mon cher.
Vulva veve.
Orchid.
Anatomies.
Isis planting Osiris.
Vital in Safed.
Veves.
Turned inside out.
Faceless beyond.
Erzulie.
Mon cher.
Ma'mbo.

Suddenly angels.
Knit from shadows.
Appear. Surround.
Hawks to another eye.
No matter what value.
Suddenly they are here.
Formal.
Taking notes.

Tongue.
Sliced into planks.
Between ryebread.
Curly-edged lettuce.
Mustard.
Stein of Ballantine Ale.

Thick instrument.
Speak before you leap.
Alphabet music.
Virtuoso.

Tongue in my mouth.
In her mouth.
Two muscles.
Tough whales.
Twine & collide.

In the beginning was breath.
Mouth.
Tongue.
A lizard peers out.

Tongue tastes and tests you
Tastes the sea
Whose creatures in blue shadow
Are history in a trace.
Neither here nor there.
The net is what tongue tastes.

She is beside me. Her tongue is all I feel. In me. There is no body but the body her tongue tastes.

She reaches in my mouth with her tongue and all my words are slowly translated into her.

She reaches her tongue into the deepest page of my throat's arc and all my words in one fast suck go streaming down her throat and become her voice.

She is beside me, her hair seaweed along my hips.

She is beside me, we are beside the tree, she is riding me, I am riding her through the Ryder night.

Tongue is faceless but when I speak it is with her voice and these are her words I am saying.

She, no longer near, remains within.

Taste your womb
Ocean whose mouthed face
Tastes of life.

Pearl tongue-tipped
At its point. Suspense
To see it either swallowed
Or drop slowly to the ground.

Moments later
A tree of mirrors
We face in ceremony.

All from a taste.

Eye.
A mystery.
Both ways.

Face. In the air. Sky.
Clouds. Face.
Face in the glass in your palm.
Plum tree blossoms. Face.
On the pillow.
Open the door. Face.
In madras curtains.
Wood grain.
Fuel oil smear.
Light socket.
Fingerprints.
Face. Awake.
Every corner.
Face.

[1972]

TREE

Take on the tree.
First, name it.
What kind of pine? Ponderosa, Pinyon, Sugar?
Outside my window. All the time. But who knows its name, right now, when I need it?

* * *

Take in the tree.
First held me in its crib. I dreamt of forests.

* * *

My nerves resemble its root system pulled out. Held up to candlelight.

* * *

The tree lives within me. In a kind of frenzy. Each pane bears branches with birds & birdnests on every stalk.

* * *

Take off the tree.
Circle by circle. Repeating hoops. Track time. The center core returns us to the mystery we travel in circles to solve.

* * *

Tree as muse informs me of my rites.

* * *

Tree in & tree out. Seek the poet to wed them.
If weeds were also trees, we would still be monkeys truer to words than most other men. Marching at chain's end. Tin cup filled with blood.

* * *

Tree trunk stored with data. Information. Tree-nation imprints. Circular merkabic wheels.
We ride in circles against the edge of limitation.
Who's got time to stop nothing. It goes on. With or without.
Line of tree time. Center tube. Pillar wood. Wheels out. Around.
Tree comes back as a question everyone asks me.

* * *

Trees walking. You & me.
Stroll the baby in a wicker buggy [elm] down Fern Road.

* * *

Tree as a machine in grade-school textbooks.

Gears, stems & stalks. V.U. needles waving back & forth.

Tree as machine. A process that leads to product.

Animated sequence. Beneath the bark we see floors filled with offices & tiny workers working day & night in the tree factory.

Only man can make a machine.

* * *

Books. Matching trees. Rest against & upon each other.

Papyri stacked to the stars. Books as stairs.

Matching trees imprinted. Rest upon each other. Ghost lovers in layers. Shelved on oak planks. Next to a table. Ghost of another tree. Upon floor slats torn from another tree. Wood walls painted monk-white. Redwood ceiling beams.

I live in the center of a tree.

A ghost among ghosts.

* * *

Tree reminds of light.
Itself between it.

* * *

Branchings. Splendor. Victory. Mercy.
Kingdom. Foundation. Beauty. Geburah.
To look up to the end of a redwood. Sunlight blinds.

* * *

Start with 10. End with 10.
Let the zeros couple into infinity.
You're left with two ones.

* * *

From a firm inner center. Spilt forth all the sun & starlight I could master. Pulse stopped. My eyes turned into the letter they looked upon.

From a firm center. Here in my fore-head, there in my aft-head. Here & there together. Up & down my spine. Spilt forth sunlight & starlight. Mustered for a moment. For a moment I saw nothing.

They say my eyes opened three weeks later. The first thing I asked for was for more.

* * *

Bolinas,
1971

LIGHTS
For JRW

Lights.
Not roses.
Blood in the shadows. Windows shut. Lace blinds drawn.
It begins to snow.
My words darken light.
Parking lights shine back in the dead doe's eye.
Eye-light I bring back to the page. A group of words flint & spark. Firelight of vision's aspect. Brought back.
Lights.
Moses pulls out. Starts it all over again.
Stares at the night sky. Bright stars on the page.
Lilith looks down at sidewalks all her life.
We are on the run through lights to light.

* * *

Turn of light.
Spotlight. Flash-freezes her face.
She opened her mouth to sing a winter song.
Drops of blood. Turn black on the snow.

* * *

Light show.
Moths dying against [upon] TV lights.
You beat your head upon a wall of lights. Nightly.
3 daughters [3 mothers] 3 white moths with golden centers. They re-charge in the sun. Under poetry's moon. As I dream it.
Yet 3 lights grow dim.
They are drawn out of themselves. Into nowhere. Into currents of electricity that enter in & out of walls. Humming light. They feed neon signs. Orders blink on & off.
3 daughters. 3 mothers. 3 ores. Permutants. Tranced into fool's gold. Light sucked out of them. They fade away. Become TV ectoplasm. Hovering over madras-covered pillows. Sunlight shines through them.
3 daughters. 3 mothers. 3 Japanese fans. 3 flipbooks of apache dancers.
Daughters of the dark. Moths to light. So light-filled they are white clouds. Up there. Against the blue. Cold.
Coaxial. Hooked into darkness. Nobody talks. Everybody battery-run.
3 daughters. 3 mothers. Shine flashlights on the ceiling. Walls. Floor. Under the covers. In the closet. Shine the light until the battery runs down.

* * *

Roll light into the roller. Type darkness.
Roll light. Bite into it.
Coffee, black.
Red Star cigarette.
Talk aur with pals in Hollywood.
B's wife, B, suicided.
We visit B in the livingroom of his wife's death. Death lingers in every corner. Her breath in each object. It leaps out of a book I open. Her name on the page.
A woman, a daughter, a mother, a poet. Murdered herself. Sleeps from the dark sphere into the light sphere. In our speech. Of earth.
We try to bring back light & form. Cognac.
The living have no way to speak to death.
Even in a book "aur" is black.
Black are the lines of Tree. Its triangles. The crown uttering light which is never seen. All on a page.
Her shoes on the floor. Next to a guitar. Overturned.
Words obliterate light while leading to its source.
An ashtray on the desk with broken cigarettes she smoked yesterday.
We hide words in light. To make light real on the page.
Seed white fields with white words.
Blood drains out. Heaven's white fluids soak into the page.
Coffee, black. Cognac. Cigarette a red star. Talking aur in Hollywood. Aur as embraced by the ether. Sparks.
Three poets. In a room in transit. The fourth is dead. A suicide. Embraces us.
All on a page.
Words to obliterate light.

* * *

Imagination electricals shake the floor.
Wires hump in space. Burning snakes.
Light-fists shake.
Tin-foil thunder roars.
Imagination thrives on dark. Invents light to lead everyone in & out of darkness. Invents imagination. Invents dark.
The parting darkness.
The opening light.

* * *

Coined word:
Image Nation.
Nation of image icons stacked-up like junked cars. To the sky.
Nation hooked. Lanced by image.
Nation of image-hungry peas. Nested in sleepingbag pods. Watching science-fiction movies on TV.

* * *

In darkness I invent light. In light I invent dark. Light compress. Worn around my head. A band pushing against the temples. Makes me see stars.

* * *

One.

Invited to dine at a dinner in death's honor.
The shape of a poem is a plate.
An engraved card reads: "Bring only yourself."
How many letters concealed in a period that ends a line?
Last of the line. A period on her plate. Bottom of a white bowl her silver spoon dips into.

* * *

Two.

On pure chance. He placed his last dime. For the last time. And won. He couldn't stop.
So he invented a philosophy: When you give up your luck changes.
He told the other gamblers. They weren't impressed.
"Crave dark?" he asked a young man perched on the edge of a ledge that led to the sea & sharp rocks.
"My luck's no good. It never has been," said the kid. Opened his arms to fly as far as life would take him.
"Go ahead. You're better off dead. Cheat life."
The kid stopped. Quit death right on the spot.
They walked back to a casino where the kid lost every cent the philosopher won back.
Life doesn't make any sense.

* * *

Three.

Ghosts are my story.
Every mirror I look into shows me a ghost.
Lovers are ghosts. Dreams confuse their faces, shapes, the smell of their bodies.
Our lady looks up.
"What are you thinking about?"
Ghost of a child. A smoke in space.
Mirror shows me. Old hat. Hello.
Hello, old ghost. Goodbye, child.
Each ghost has a story. Unfolding packet of snapshots.
Jew is ghost.
Ghost factories serenade us with history.
Ghost gloves are strong around my neck.
They snap off the lights.

* * *

Take light seriously.

Shineth down upon my cracked head. Hair & boneshell gasoline in the sunrise.

Darts of Bram Stoker hits bull. Crying colors of c. 1900 lithographs. Masonic. Rosicrucian.

Alight. The lift that bulbs the Ainsof.

Listening to the tusk radio. Ambulance lights orbit above.

* * *

ALL THAT BREATHES SHALL PRAISE THE LORD.
PRAISE YE THE LORD!
And all His angels. Collide in space. For favor at the feast.
Fight for food as the master eats the universe.
Here, a splinter of a planet for you. O Isaac.
Here, a crumb of the sun for you. O Shamshiel.
Here, a drop of water holding a thousand mysteries. O Raziel.
Here, a necklace of glaciers. O Ithuriel.
Here, a crust of nova. O Rampel.
Sparrows & tohees at the Tzaddik's table. Hop about.
Tigers & cows. Spiders & ladybugs. Ants & Onoel, the donkey, at the wonder-worker's bench.
Kildeer & ibis turn the pages of our book.
Ain. Ain Sof. Ain Sof Aur.
In the Name is the garden contained within a wound.
Praise ye the Lord.
Loon thee O holy One.
Wing away dawn's curtain.
Dawn thee O light of revelation.
Dance with the Bride.
Shall we not all dance the round?
Feather. Fur. Fin. Flesh.
All toe to the same tone.
No more numbers.
Goodbye ghosts. Hope the angel says hello.

* * *

Frost-light breaks into rainbows that slowly slip off the last living white rose in our backyard garden.

* * *

Bolinas,
1971

CRACKS
For Jack

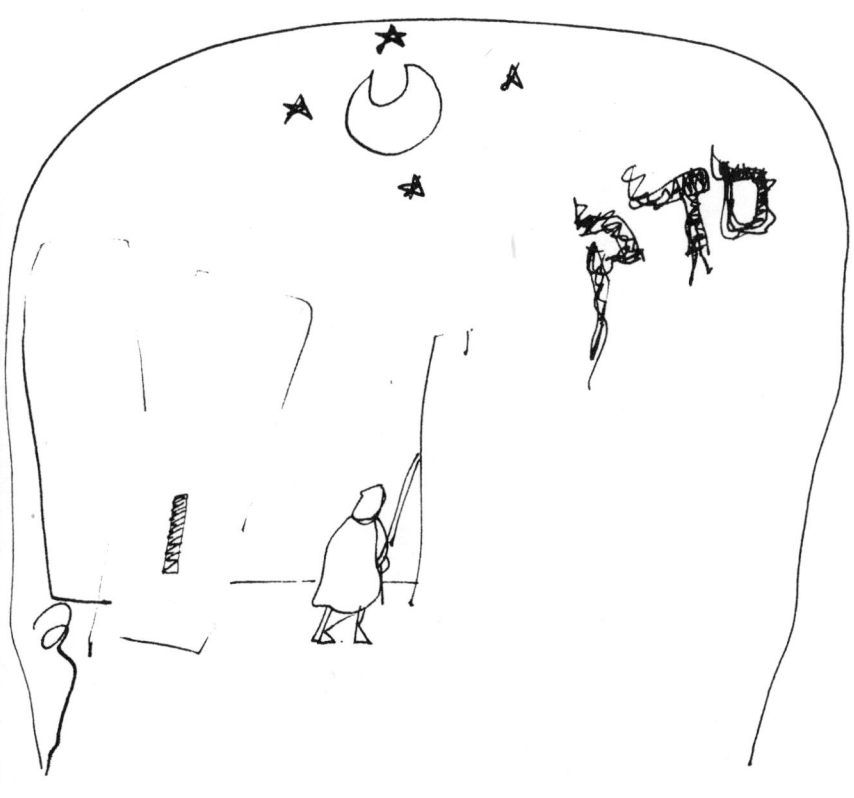

Kabbalah is receiving. To receive. Receiver.
In [upon] entering begins the twists & turns.

* * *

Bumper-sticker, left hand, next to cryptic license plate announces:
"EVIL" IS "LIVE" BACKWARDS.
The license: KBL AUT AUR 10.
No kidding.
Would the poem kid?
Would the kid kid?
Kid gets dizzy in the backyard. Goat chewing off the baby's arm. Would that be funny, backwards or forwards?

* * *

For word.
Back the word. Back it up. Give it backing.
Word sees itself. All around. As we do. Looks for itself on every page.

* * *

The face of a word reversed.

Hold a page to light. Shining through all letters. Scrambling them.

They turn backwards & forwards. Light holds me up. My faces reversed. Turned inside-out.

Lightbulb hangs from the ceiling of a 69th Street room. I eat peyote. 3 days & 3 nights. Scrambled. Everything. Backwards & forwards.

I read & write poems I can not kid.

My eyes hang out of my skull to see.

When I was 19.

But now I am 35. "And you're still alive." Sings Joe Turner. *Old Maid Blues*. 1947. Savoy.

No more peyote. I go against the grain.

Tribe needs itself to grow fat. Feed itself all the arms & legs it can. Tribe needs itself for food. Eats whatever it gets.

Everyone in America talks about eating.

Overfed, everyone is hungry.

After the first toke the tapeworm stirs.

Token-food. Fed into subway turnstiles. Now 35 cents. When I was a peyote eater it was only 10 cents.

The subway eats itself up. The people inside devour each other. Ten enter a car. Perhaps only five leave. Alive.

The five survivors are full. But hungry again as they walk up stairs to the sidewalk, the sky.

* * *

Only the living laugh.
Chaplin as Hitler.
It is not theatre. You're right. It's "video evil". Certainly not vaudeville.
Not Vau. Vou. Satan. Natal comet. Stage rising up from the Roxy basement.
Artaud wanted the stage to eat the audience alive. Devour them into reply. Responsiveness. Alive-ness. Nothing more or less.
But you're right.
TV cuts the cords. The knots. The nerves. The words. The touch. Cuts into it all.
TV means "Transvestite" in sex want-ads.
Glass page. We can not turn off.
Turn the pages.
Takes word away.
Living from reel to reel.
"Nothing is real," sings a Beatle.

* * *

I'm told again to read Buber.
"[Buber] makes clear the weight & dimension of spirit ecology. Evil needs God as a balance. Yin-Yang. Evil is the wheel that holds the chariot up. All parts depend on each other."
TV cuts the cords.
No resistance. Gone.
No matter how long your hair grows, we have been cut off at the roots.

* * *

Evil interchangeable in Kabbalah.
Starts in the blood or sperm. Microbe or atom. Light bending to the eye from a space words can not link to.
Live evil like the other impulses. Punched into loops. Extended through. Printed on. Moebius ribbons. Nerve ends. Blood alphabet intestines.
When evil is isolated it is the mask of power.
Power is always used against the heart,
Power is against the word.

* * *

The Police are outside looking in.

We are inside. Watching TV.

Some cops still wear leather boots. Others wear bright blue vinyl Eisenhower jackets. Silver buttons. Brass bullets in wide cowhide X's strapped around their chests.

We are inside. Watching TV. Watching the President pull down a screen. War home movies.

War theatre. War fair. War games. Tour of duty. One Star. Two Star. Three Star. Four Star. Five Star. Generals.

Other cops are tall & slender like cowboys. Taut. They are in charge of machine guns. They keep better score. I don't know why.

We are popping corn.

Other cops are traditional. Bred that way. Squat men. Bellys hang over gun belts. They are called many affectionate yet insulting names. In smokey rooms awards are given to officers who have distinguished themselves in duty. Awards to widows who endure & survive the duty. Placques & medals to sons & daughters who will sire the future.

We watch men in topcoats. News. They grab demonstrators by the hair. Kick them in the spinal base. Policemen start clubbing others caught off-guard by the men in topcoats. They are secret Government agents. They serve under a trilogy of initials. They have neat parts in their hair. You never notice them. Suddenly they are all over the place. Men in topcoats. Killers who look like highschool principals.

* * *

Evil is re-invented every day. On TV. Nobody believes in it any more.

Unless it is sensational. Unless it touches the body. But even then.

We will be policeman. Watching ourselves on TV. Enforcing law in the streets.

Law spelled backwards. What we're up against.

* * *

Kaballah pilfered by Lilith's dancers.
The inside magic taken outside where it is used against the body.
What they call magic is another kind of oppression.
Control. Fever. Ownership. Dominion. Real estate.
None of these words mean "to receive."

      *   *   *

Kabbalah pilfered in Hollywood labs.
Final. Eternal. Nothing dies. Hide the mirror. Time won't win.
Records, posters, greetingcards.
Mail orders. Each day I open envelopes for direction.
Rabbi Judah Loew of Prague made the Golem out of Moldau clay. Backwards.
Hebrew is backwards.
What does the double speak?
Orpheus & Heurtebise went backwards to Hades for her.
Poets give words back.
Words give back poets.
All this goes on. The pilfer continues. Green radium. Bubbles. Dry ice garage. Late show. Boris & Bela. Masks. Manson. Son of man. Backwards. A Bomb.
A-Bomb. The first. 300,000 die in its light. Aleph.
A-Bomb. Its light gives birth to TV.

      *   *   *

Today TV tells us. Hanoi is ready to sign a peace pact. Two weeks from Election Day, U.S.A.
There is no evil left to take hold of. It slides out of reach. Into the next show.
Assassins dreams the same dreams as Presidents.
Would the word. Has the word. Failed?
I don't care how many starlets Kissinger fucks.
Would the word. Has the word. Failed?
Kissinger of death.

* * *

They keep trying to rob us of mystery. The video devils. The vid grids. Grid the kid. Pin him down. Trying to rob us of mystery our words robe.
You are forced to read license plates.
Watching the 10 o'clock News destroys me.
They keep trying to rob mystery of mystery. Turn everything into a movie. We want to be larger than darkness.

* * *

Wherever. Anywhere. A letter emerges. We shall love it. Robe it. Disrobe it. Follow it wherever it goes. Into the next letter. The next. The next.

If it's a net the quest snares us with, don't be nettled. We seek marvels anywhere a letter emerges.

* * *

Tina's driving to the A&P.
I tell her I take letters seriously.
She thinks I read too much into your last letter. Where you say:
"This will be the last word till you get across."

* * *

In Odessa. I awake with the rooster. Lay tifillin. Unwrap the Torah. Read from it. Pray. Clothe the Torah.

Enter a room overlooking an alley. Every afternoon a fiddler beggar comes to feed me lunch.

There. Here. Then and now. I sit before a piece of white paper.

I seek the letters of my name. My soul. I want to crack apart the knots of silence binding my brain.

In Brooklyn. I wake with the radiator. Steam-alarm. Clank. Rattle.

Steamy window wiped dry of diamonds. Snow outside on the cement backyard.

I dive into the snow. Roll upon its soft body. Snow is paper. The marks my body makes on snow we call Angels.

Back inside. I mark letters on blue lines of a Spiral Notebook. Trying to write the history of everything. From the beginning to the end. To discover the letters of my name. My soul.

There. Here. Then or now.

* * *

10 O'Clock News.
Gangsters. Check into a New Jersey courthouse. One puts a black handkerchief over his face. Hooded. Black band across the eyes. Naked men & women. Caught.
The Lone Ranger. Hooded. Cowled. Assassins at a midnight rite.
Sacred words are murmured. Traditional designs drawn on the floor. The ceiling. Black satin curtains on the walls. Over the windows.
Instead of a sword, it is a silencer. Magnum. Slid across the table top.
They bring in a person. Shrouded white. Target practise. Begins.
10 O'Clock News.
Embezzler covers his face with both hands. Handcuffed. A mourner.
Kissinger. Flanked by men in topcoats. In between flights. Announces a settlement with South Vietnam.
President Nixon rubs fingerprints against his 5 O'Clock shadow. His fingertips spark white bulletins. He reassures everyone that everything is under control.

* * *

When they operate. It is miles of teletype. Pulled out of the patient.

Garbage is used to block up holes in the walls.

Rats eat it. On their way out. To eat you.

You lay on a pallet of *N.Y. Times*.

Each day the janitor drags you up another flight of stairs. Soon you'll be in the pigeon coop on the roof.

You lay on a pallet of *N.Y. Times* on a linoleum floor. Cage bars rattle. Cockroaches. Surround you.

Two junkies. Try to get in. Even though they see you on the floor. Cockroaches pulling teletype out of your mouth. Even though they see you, they do not care. They are without fear. It makes no difference. But their hands can not function with skill. One tears a fingernail off his finger trying to get in. Bends over in silent agony.

When the sun shines everyone ducks.

* * *

It's called junk. Or shit. Or stuff.
It's white. Red blood mixes with it.
It's a talc to keep machines in tact.
We lose sight.
Chemical control.
Feed the dealers.
Dealer never uses the stuff. Junk. Shit.
Money his fix.
Junkies need money to fix.
They are always too late.
Stuff. Shit.
The next moment it is junk.
The stuff we were told to buy last week is now junk. The stuff stacks up. We're stuck with it. All of it. Stick it into our arms to get rid of it. Blood. We are told to buy. From the beginning. To buy ourselves to death. Buy. Sell. It is never new enough. It is never old enough.
It is shit. Stuff. Inert.
Indestructible plastics wash up on all the shores. Plastic coffins we store death inside of.
Artists ride white light.
It is called horse.
Ride into night.
Shit. Junk. Stuff.
Ride into the White House. Chip your fix off the dome.
Junk is light's enemy. It is not evil.
There is no evil. There is no good. There is only junk.
Turn on your set. Plug in.

* * *

Kaballah is receiving. What arises from the junk.
Kaballah is how we resist junk.
Kaballah is beyond us.
Within everything.
Sustains.
Holds.
Allows.
In [upon] entering begins the twists & turns.

     *   *   *

         Bolinas—Stamford,
         1971-1972

APPLE

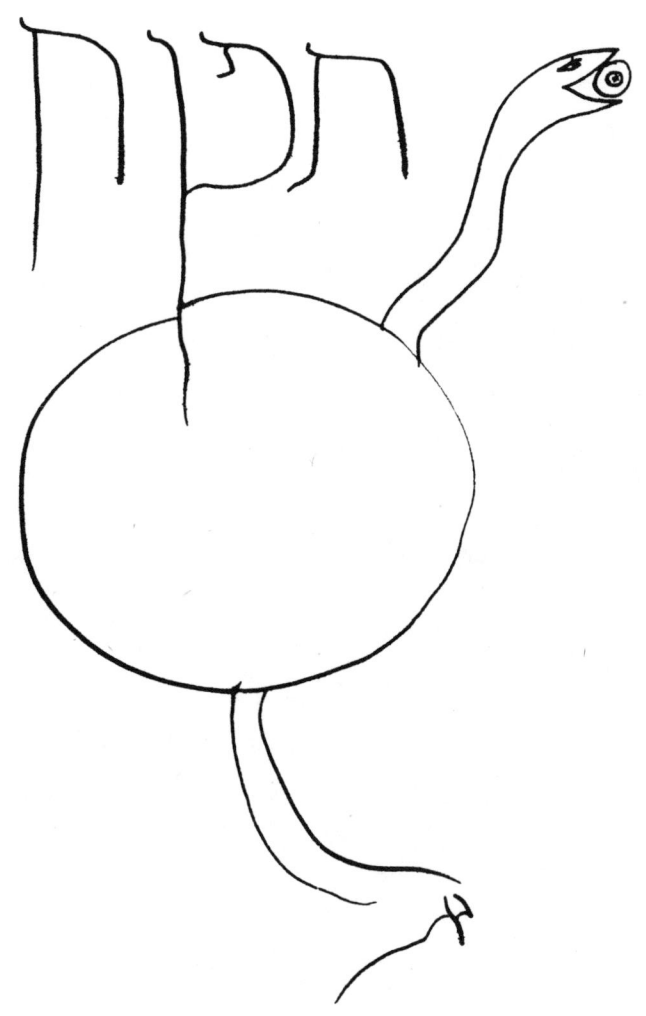

1.

Fall, 1972

Branched,
partial,
broken

how I ramble in mid-noon

earthly garden
heavenly garden

imagination
soil
flats of soul
sprouts set out in her
greenhouse

tentative shoots
explore moist yellow heat
with bright green
tongues uncurling.

A bird above the glass
above the roofs
sings of lives
shadowed in the garden.
Fences of heaven.

●

Adam the page.
Apple: language.
Serpent the poem.
Eve the book.

       •

Pools of Adam
Streams of Eve
Lakes and rivers
Moral dreams float upon.

Lilies, bull-rushes
Vibrating lotus
Giant frog kings ride.

Their green mouths
Open to speak
Radio.

•

Upright serpent
    First professor
Walked talk
    Into the circle
Brought forth
    Discourse
Argument
    Taught balances
Heads   tales
    Both sides of a word
Where before
    Everything was present
Without past or future.

•

Michael calls long-distance from Seattle.
He's left his wife.
They have one child,
A son, she will keep.
Michael says it's still raining
In Seattle, winter won't quit.
A disc in the center of his spine
Has slipped. Amulet
Ripped off bedstead.
Who comes forth with magical psalm?
Bleached sheets
Strangle in Bolinas wind
Outside the kitchen window.

•

Out of shared unequal ground
A garden faces me.
I can't erase the invisible.
Yet you are there in green
Rooted within a dark ark of radium
Shielding our kids from falling angels.

•

2.

Commentary, 1974

I make an apple out of an alphabet.
I put it together in panels of round sheets. Each sheet has a letter on one side and red skin on the other side.
It is held together by sugar glue.
It's meant to be eaten, all of it, the seeds as well.
When it is inside it will be only a matter of time before its broken parts begin to sprout, re-shape and cohere.

*

Yeshouah's grey cheeks. The sheet's pulled down.
His nose sparkles with frost.
Hands folded over bruised chest.
Damaged ankles. Pubic hairs a white field.
Blue tinted genitals. Dreaming of clouds.

When they break into the chest cavity they find two large black apples where his lungs should be.

They find his spine is composed of apple seeds.

When they empty his blood it is golden colored like apple juice. Red flakes like ash float up to the top of their jars.

*

ap . ple / 'ap - l / n. *often attrib*
[ME *appel*, fr. OE *aeppel*; akin to
OHG *apful* apple, OSlav *abluko*] 1:
the fleshy usu. rounded and red
or yellow edible pome fruit of a
tree (genus *Malus*) of the rose
family . . .

*

Edible pome, the poem in its bulb of sleep, a rose.
I fashion my apple in a garden by the sea of freeways.
   A peach tree, lemon tree, apple tree, plum tree, lined in a straight row, bordered by tall alarms of bamboo shading leaves mulched around each tree's base. Fennel plumes; Scotch broom yellow buds awake.
   I sit like my grandfather's father in Kiev, on the ground, legs folded, sewing together my apple.

*

Without digressing, Mom's apple pie.

Generations of Kabbalah erased in the kitchen, the national desert of America.

Not to be unpious but to continue nevertheless:

                      Road-wrinkled trucker sits at Hi-Way Eats with a cup of java, joe, & a piece of apple pie à la mode served by Cindy Jo Flint whose people have been making baking frying broiling food for truckers since the Highway went thru the beginning and end of the Depression.

        Or apple turn-over
        or apple Betty
        or apple strudel
        or apple sauce.

The maiden like a boa coils & uncoils around historic intrigues; apple-jack cooked in political kitchens served in buffed brass goblets.

Here, eat.

You know the joke:

                    A Jewish gangster shot full of holes stumbles, crawls, drags his bloody self crosstown to the Lower East Side to the old tenement block he was born on. Up the stairs, slowly, painfully, bleeding buckets of Yiddish theatre on each step. Finally gets to Momma's door & scrapes on it with bloody fingers. Momma opens the door, looks down at her son, says, "Shhh. Eat now, talk later."

Then there's the whole pig whose mouth is stuffed with the whole apple.
An apple a day keeps the Doctor away.
Deep-dish hot apple pie served in Hollywood drive-ins.
Candied apples sold at carnivals, amusement parks. The red glaze tastes of Pepsodent, the caramel like rootbeer.
Apple the corporation founded by Beatles.
Apple in Latin means evil.

*

—As I eat so am I eaten.
The slow talker begins.
—Where I go so have I been.
—Where in the sky is my eye.
—Where in the bone is my mouth.
—So it is proven, it still remains secret.
—Slowly I walk, gathering speed, until I fly.

The slow talker walks beyond the range of microphones into a valley of apple trees where each bough houses a resident serpent who is jade green with an active but silent pink forked tongue which decorates the sweet air of remembered Paradise.

*

Paradise, the garden, PaRDeS, the anagram, pre-coded in the lights of our creation.

Sperm prophets in radiant rockets explode into her pink sea.

When I remember being born I remember the pink light torn away to reveal the green hum of trees.

How easy the transition from world to world. Above my wide awake eyes clouds unfurl banners engraved with Merkabic proclamations. Nations and states of sky peopled by tribal comets congregate beneath the phosphorescent apple of the moon still visible in the veils of daylight blue space.

Either way.

Either from her clay or from her belly ocean, I enter into the next round of lights and I'm repaired and blank, all senses unworked, alert to all signs. Music of speech and song woven into a basket I am rocked in. Into and out of sleep, the dream, paradise.

Child within apple darkness sucks out the last light and in the next moment will be re-born, his memory carried from meadow to meadow in the folds of a goldfinch's wings.

No alarm.

The child greets an enormous world ensphered in Paradise.

We meet in the middle of a philosophical road. In space or in a specific grove. Neither here nor there. One foot in, one foot out. We meet and recognize each other. Again and again.

*

Eve's dugs solemnly lay against her ancient chest. Her skin white as the storm of thin white hairs sprouting from her baby-pink skull.

—It's utterly useless to sing another song to the child. My children are up & out; they are gone. They are grown. Their children are grown.

—The children keep growing until their faces, crushed by time, are pushed backwards into the anonymous child-face. The gravity of oncoming death replaces the face it erases with the face of a child.

—The children keep growing up. They enter new ether; their faces & bodies transform to suit the higher climate, to move within the refined light.

—The children grow up; they grow beyond bones & skin. Their eyes, their mouths, grow sure to the touch of glass between us.

*

The artist, more than others, hopes to put the apple back together as it was before the first bite.

*

Evangelist of childhood lore, Johnny Appleseed, takes great form with his Yod & Aleph, his fecundating obsession to apple-tree the entire North American continent. Scattering seed wherever he goes.

Yeshouah was not nailed to an apple tree yet many believe Christos was the New Adam and Mary the New Eve and when she holds an apple in her hands it is the fruit of salvation.

New Adam the son, New Eve the mother & Johnny Appleseed hitching all over America scattering seeds in a movie ballet, a sequence repeated as the pages of a day-to-day calendar turn, are torn off, turn, torn off. In the movie of Johnny's myth, Walt Disney Yahweh concocts remote bestiaries in rooms of new Eden Disneyland, Burbank art racks where Disney artists in popcorn cells draw each step, each breath, this Johnny Appleseed takes. Scattering seed wherever he goes.

New Adam, New Christ, New Eve, New Mary, and from this union a larger-than-life postage stamp of Johnny Appleseed returns after years of Dharma-bumming thru time in cahoots with the Wizard of Menlo. This Yod-Aleph leans against an iron lamp-post in Berkeley hitching North to anywhere. He holds a cardboard sign out to automobiles, trucks.

Scattering seed wherever he goes.

*

An alarming feast.
She licks her lips.
He feels apple fragments freeze in his throat. Dry ice.
Her eyes change colors.
He tries to speak. Plants die in the frost of his breath.
I sit in the backyard making an apple and threading pieces of paper onto the branches of fruit trees.

I'm attaching poems to tree branches like Japanese do; like the Hebrews, I'm throwing my words back into earth.

I scribble moments on paper and toss them into the compost pit.

I open a book, dive in, press myself inside it, shut the lid. I will soon dry between the pages, a shape of time.

There are rainbows for the moment along edges of black printing ink in ridged imprints of type deep in the paper's weave.

*

—I was all right before the first bite
Now illusion pains me as much as hope.

*

Loss of nature. Our part in its every moment.

No matter how or what I say, nature hears nothing, she turns away from books.

I make an apple whose inside layers are coded with notes of bird-songs. In darkness I play a tape of forest birds, jungle birds, arctic birds. Their songs alter night I lie within. Music colors the canopy, the shelter, with veins of light my ear tries to order.

But I lose focus. Newton's use of me broken.

*

—*Who would see the apple would see only a part of its face.*
The moon reserves the same right of vision.
But we who work thru things, we worm folk, late-night moth phantasms, we deserve the full edge of what our vision tests daily.
It is always brought back as we now understand light bends to a page or a screen or a leaf.
That there is no end indicates, therefore, that there is no beginning and, thus, any apple seen from any side is as much of the apple as is possible.

So speaketh the Rabbi who, it is said, sits enthroned in a wheelchair behind a wall where ideas turn into centuries of mystery and the tears of seekers become a cement to hold the wall upright against all intruders.

It is said in whispers that his wheelchair is perfectly ordinary-looking until, by some holy rigamarole, the Rabbi activates it to carry him wherever it is he wants to go.

According to some who have peeked between their fingers which should have been held over the eyes, the wheelchair is transformed into a chariot which rises slowly, dramatically, above ordinary earth and seeks its proper station at the gate of the first heaven. We are blessed that the Rabbi is content to commute between ordinary earth and the first heaven.

Sha, he is about to speak again.

*

Electric skin of serpent ghost is flashing paper for the book of death, an hysterical foil devouring pens and pencils.

Snake whips of yanked-out spines and nervous systems.

Wise guy.

When I open my mouth in murder's darkness it is snake who thrusts words out into night.

Each finger I put against love's curve turns cobra.

Mercedes limousine waits outside.

Lady of plagiarized fur waits inside it smoking African cigarettes, immaculate.

I say goodbye to love in ten terrible scars.

Snake smoke out of the pistol's burnt mouth.

Snake of all seasons, one after the other, twelve loops of ascension. But I get nowhere. I keep going in circles to the center which keeps widening.

Snake foundation holds the house up.

Snake in the hand of a believer. One in each fist.

*

The work piles up. Letters to answer, bills. Apples whose weight in the wind proves too hard for the branch fall onto the ground. The sun and rain and moon radiation turns the pages into brown brittle fragments. A questionable mulch for the tree.

The apple is layers of itself.
I approach it like sculpture. But, no, in truth, I go at it one dimension at a time, like papier maché or as if I were really making an onion.
The glue I use varies and depends upon what's near, also, honestly, what I can afford from day to day.
You would think the construction of an apple would cost next to nothing. I and you and the others are wrong.

Enterprise, they would build an earth out of your praises.

*

I can't tell you how long it takes to make an apple. It depends on who's shaping it. For myself, the apple remains half done. Perhaps that's enough. There are no books on the subject, no masters. If it has been tried before there are no records of the attempt.

—And what would you do with your apple when you finished it? Bronze it? Or take Polaroid color instant snapshots of it? Anyway who would believe if you made it right that you actually made it? And what happens when it starts to rot? Could you eat it?

My one and only student, a half-breed from the projects, hangs around to watch me fall.

—It would be easier to grow an apple tree than to make your own apple, he says. He sounds like the Rabbi.

The snake, voiceless, uses his body to imprint letters & words on dusty roads leading out of Eden.

*

The ending is a thread pulled out of the stem which unravels the book.

Its leaves are caught in light and scatter upwards like kites.

   A few pages, a few letters, are left on the ground and I set about to make another apple.
   When they ask me all I can say is that after the first creation the momentum becomes natural and to be without a simple task is to be without meaning, without a name.

*

Oakie Hill,
Tewksbury Heights,
California.
1975 / 5735-36.

POST-CARTE

These six works reflect my involvement with Kabbalah and mark a further attempt to integrate some of its patterns and symbols into my work.[1] The pieces can be read with or without the following clues and allusions, additions and subtractions.

I salute the banner of those who avoid all introductions, prefaces, prologues, epilogues, etc. The spirit once within a corpse is long gone by the time a flag is wrapped around its stiff forgery.

For the others whose focus demands constant footnotes, annotations, verifications, etc., may I announce that I'm passing through your suburbs riding the Twentieth Century Limited to the edge of America and, for the most part, am unavailable for interrogation.

* * *

---

1. "The Golem Wheel" in *Dark Continent* [Oyez, Berkeley, 1967]; *Yesod* [Trigram Press, London, 1969]; *Knots* [Tree Books, Bolinas, 1971]; *Hero/Lil* [Black Sparrow Press, Los Angeles, 1973]; *The Eyes, The Blood* [Mudra, Berkeley, 1974;] "From A Midrash" in *Tens: Selected Poems, 1961-1971* [McGraw-Hill Book Company, New York, 1973.]

1] VAV

Sixth letter of the Hebrew Alphabet.
On the sixth day man was created according to Genesis.
The Seraphim in Isaiah had six wings. The visions of Isaiah and Ezekiel form the basis of Merkabah mysticism, forerunner of mystical speculative inquiry which later developed into Kabbalah.
It is the letter like the angel which announced itself during the writing of the poem.
Angels appear like flies. Like ghosts. They enter your room.
Angels appear and disappear. To some they are sparks to guide acts of creation, they illuminate the page. X-rays of the poem which like laser beams reveal words hidden within paper. They are muse.
To others, angels float in metaphysical dawn skies to be shot down like mallards. Many do not believe angels exist. Some only want them to dance on the tip of a pin.
Vav is the Hebrew ideogram for peg or nail.
According to the 19th century French scholar of occult matters, Fabre d'Olivet—"VAV: This character offers the image of the most profound, the most inconceivable mystery, the image of the knot which unites, or the point which separates nothingness and being. It is the universal, convertible sign which makes a thing pass from one nature to another . . ." [*The Hebraic Tongue Restored and the True Meaning of the Hebrew Words Re-established and Proved by their Radical Analysis.* G.P. Putnam's Sons, New York and London, 1921. "Done into English by Nayán Louise Redfield"]
Carlo Suarès, a contemporary Qabalist (his spelling), tells us that Vav "expresses the fertilizing agent, that which impregnates." [*The Cipher of Genesis: The*

Original Code of the Qabala as applied to The Scriptures. Shambala Publications, Incorporated, Berkeley, 1970.]

Vav is the third letter of the Tetragrammaton: YHVH. Between two Hays. It is a Yod-holding staff, crowned by Yod. Yod and Vav become ithyphallic glyphs of immediate and cosmic transmission.

Vav between two Daleths: DVD. Which is also my name. Vav the angel in the center of my name whose numbers add up to five, Hay.

But all this is plain enough.

What about Vav the angel responsible for the poem of his name?

He never returned to write another poem through me, though he later allowed his image to move through my pen into the drawings which accompany the text.

I now see him in the eyes of others. Friends, strangers.

Angels are a multitude even though they bless us one at a time. If I limit their number to twenty-two, each named after a letter from the Hebrew Alphabet, Gustav Davidson has catalogued thousands in his marvelous *A Dictionary of Angels* [The Free Press, New York, 1967].

Many poets seek and are guided by their signifying angel. Angels are sometimes confused as doubles.

Vav is the number six which is the title of this book.

Moving light around a poet's head. Dawned in his devotions. Wings of creation meet midway in the sky like the male hummingbird in soaring expression of love. Angels all. Bards in white or feathered shamans. Shimmying up the sky-pole to the next dream, the new poem.

* * *

The work is dedicated to Jim Willems who often resembles the angel in more ways than the poem does.

2] FACE

An attempt to work with the concept of *Parzuf*.

"Each of [the] *Sefirot* is constructed of ten Lights, each of which in turn is composed of an equal number of Lights . . . *ad infinitum*. When . . . only a single Light [is illuminated in one of these vessels] it is called a *Sefira*. When all the Lights in a vessel are illumined then it is defined as a *Parzuf* (Person). In order that it may be called a complete and perfect *Parzuf*, every division within must shine with all its Light so that the number of Lights will total six hundred and thirteen—the number of parts in a man's body. Only then is it considered complete.

"There are but five *Parzufim* (Persons) . . . for not every *Sefira* of the ten had the power to radiate in the manner just described. Only *Kether, Hokmah, Binah* and *Malkuth* could do so. They are called:

'ARIK ANPIN (Macroprosopus—*Kether*
ABA and IMA (Mother and Father)—
    Hokmah and *Binah*
and
NUKBA (the Feminine Polarity)—
Malkuth.

". . . the six remaining *Sefirot, Hesed, Gevurah, T'fereth, Nezach, Hod* and *Yesod*, did not have the individual power to radiate as forcefully as the others. Collectively . . . these lost six *Sefirot* build up a *Parzuf*; it is called ZEIR ANPIN (Microprosopus) . . .

". . . the first *Parzuf* . . . manifested in the worlds was Adam Kadmon (Primordial Man); all the subsequent stages and the *Parzufim* resulted from him. He is united with the

Emanator Himself and is very much concealed. We cannot say anything whatsoever about the Primordial Man, but can treat only of the branches that ramify from him to the outside.

"From this Primordial Man come many worlds—worlds without number . . . 'Seeing,' 'Hearing,' 'Smell' and 'Speech' . . . They issue from the *eyes*, from the *ears*, from the *nose* and from the *mouth* of Adam Kadmon." [*General Principles of The Kabbalah (K'Lach Pischai Chochma: 138 Openings to the Study of Kabbalah*) by Rabbi Moses C. Luzzatto. Translation by The Research Centre of the Kabbalah. The Press of The Research Centre of Kabbalah (Distributed by Samuel Weiser Inc.), New York, 1970.]

* * *

"We have learned [by oral tradition]: that the Book of Mystery is the book which describes the equilibrium of the Balance. Before the Balance existed, Face could not view Face, and the primordial kings died, and their sustenance was not found, and the earth was desolate until the Head, the Delight of all Delights, prepared, perfected and imparted the garments of costliness. This Balance hangs in the Place [*Maqom*] which is No-Thing [*Ayin*]. In the same were brought into equilibrium those who did not yet exist. The Balance exists through the At-tee'qah, i.e., Ancient One. It is not held anywhere and is invisible. In it, ascended, and in it, do ascend, things which were not, which are, and which will be. In the Concealed of the Concealed, there is formed and prepared, the representation of a cranium

(The immense cranium is the representation of the Makrokosm, the arched firmament above us and surrounding us, called [the] Heaven[s]. The Makrokosm is usually represented as an immense man, but sometimes as an immense head . . .)
full of crystalline dew, a membrane of air. Transparent and hidden filaments of pure wool are hanging in the Balance.
(Hanging threads of pure wook, are a symbol among some of the Orientals for the efflux of wisdom and vitality.)

And they manifest the Good Will of Good Wills through the prayers of the lower ones, by a look of the open eye which never sleeps and is always watching. The Providence below by the light [or eye] of the Providence above." [Portion from *Sifra D'Tzeniyutha* in *Qabbalah: The Philosophical Writings of Solomon Ben Yehuda Ibn Gebirol or Avicebron and their connection with the Hebrew Qabbalah and Sepher ha-Zohar, with remarks upon the antiquity and content of the latter, and translations of selected passages from the same. Also An Ancient Lodge of Initiates, Translated From The Zohar, And an abstract of an Essay upon the Chinese Qabbalah, contained in the book called the Yih King; a translation of part of the Mystic Theology of Dionysios, the Areopagite; and an account of the construction of the ancient Akkadian and Chaldean Universe, etc.* by Isaac Myer (1888). Samuel Weiser Incorporated, New York, 1970.]

* * * *

"Parzupheem, i.e., Faces (Visages or Aspects)." [ibid.]

* * * *

"As to the active energies of the King and Queen, whom the Qabbalists frequently term, *the Two Faces*. [Zohar, iii, fol. 10*b*.] These form an androgenic principle whose constant endeavor is to shed upon the world new life and kindness and preserve and perpetuate, under the Will of the Supreme Deity, the work of the original creation. The reciprocal affinity of the Two Faces operates in two ways [. . .] Sometimes it is from Above to Below [. . .] then the existence and life go out of the Highest World affecting the objects of nature; sometimes, on the contrary, it goes from the Below to the Above, that is from this, our world of illusion, change and unreality, to the real and true and Absolute Above; and takes back to the Highest [those] existences entitled to such a return." [ibid.]

* * *

"Before the world was created [the *Anpeen*, Faces] did not look attentively, Faces to Faces, and the primitive worlds were made without perfect formations, and therefore the primitive worlds were destroyed. [Zohar iii, 292*a* and *b*.]

* * *

The face is a light like the page. Like the page it lights the space between words which are black-cowled silhouettes moving through snowfall.

* * *

The page faces me. Face to face.
Even what can not be faced or masked or marked down.
Silhouettes. One word. A knot of words.

* * *

Or what can not be faced. Defacement. A defaced soul. The book torn out of him. The veins pulled out. Nervous system rootsystem removed. A million crows scatter upward like buckshot.

* * *

Face is incomplete. Merely prelude. Book One, Part One. The general survey of the Face is complete, but the other sections on Tongue, Eyes, Ears, Beard, Teeth, etc., remain either unwritten or in various stages of incompletion.

The work was begun in response and tribute to the process of reception introduced to me in *The Kabbalah Unveiled: Containing the following Books of the Zohar: THE BOOK OF CONCEALED MYSTERY, THE GREATER HOLY ASSEMBLY, THE LESSER HOLY ASSEMBLY; Translated into English from the Latin version of Knorr von Rosenroth, and collated with the original Chaldee and Hebrew text* by S. L. MacGregor Mathers [Originally published in London in 1927; reprinted by Samuel Weiser, New York, 1968] and *The Measure of the (Divine) Body: Shiur Qoma from The Book of the Angelic Secrets of the Great One: Sefer Raziel Hagadol;* translated by The Work of The Chariot [The Work of the Chariot, Los Angeles, n.d.].

The detailing of the Macrocosm and Microcosm, The Greater and Lesser Holy Assemblies, which report in deliberate and minute detail each inch and eternity, from toes to crown-curls, of Adam Kadmon who becomes, as the poem, a light projected inward which moves outwards on creative impulse to find ground in the tablets of a book which again returns its imprinting within. The process of creating and receiving a spark of holy energy becomes the holy energy itself.

The power of those words in the Zoharitic books matched with the condensed hints of the *Sefer Yetzirah* finally, once more, enabled me to sit still in the backyard and watch universes conduct the actual business of the poem in broad daylight.

* * *

There exists therefore the shadow of the faceless in all the words moving by. The page is emanation. Each page, sentence, word, punctuation mark, is a parzuf, a sephirotic engraving.

* * *

The work is dedicated to the language which created the original texts and to Knorr von Rosenroth and his associates Henry More and Franciscus Mercurius Van Helmont; to the magus-trickster S. L. MacGregor Mathers; to D. L. Bloxom of The Work of The Chariot.

3] TREE

Really needs little explaining.

A meditation on the Sephiroth accompanied by facets of other facts I also live with.

Sefiroth: ten emanations through which the energies

of holiness manifest themselves, become whole. A circuit of lights, a pattern of their circulation.

Sefiroth: the tree's ten branches, the man's ten fingers reach out to pull the harp's strings, shape song, sing.

* * *

The written tree and the tree in front of me.
Literal and metaphorical.

* * *

The writing took place in a room of a three-floor mammoth lodge we rented in Bolinas. Two blocks from the Pacific Ocean, yet outside my window were dense woods.

In my room I often felt surrounded by the tree, within it, concealed in its core. My world became wood extended by metals.

* * *

For allowing our family a year in his "summer cottage" I dedicate this work to Mr. Parsons of Yolo County, California.

4] LIGHTS

Light in Hebrew is *aur*.

A point that is light upon light until all self-ness or consciousness is disintegrated into a sheet of paper awaiting a word.

Last night my friend Allen Say and my wife Tina,

both former art students at the same school in Los Angeles during the same time and having the same teacher, were arguing about black and white. Allen said that all the colors of the spectrum when combined became white; Tina insisted that they all became black.

* * *

Infinite Light: *Aur Ain Soph*—"to which there [is] no beginning nor yet any end: all was Light permeating everything evenly."

* * *

Zimzum—"He contracted the light [of *Aur Ain Soph*] Himself into the middle point—in the very centre. He contracted that Light and removed Himself . . . so that in [the] . . . mid-point . . . remained an empty place . . . air . . . a void . . ." [*Tree of Life* (Luria-Vital). Work of the Chariot, Los Angeles, 1970.]

* * *

5] CRACKS

En route to London, driving through USA with my wife, our three daughters, visiting (we thought for the last time) key friends across America: the Bermans and the Hirschmans in LA, the Brakhages in Colorado, the Brandis in New Mexico, Howard Schwartz in St Louis, Larry Fagin in Manhattan. Our plan was to leave and never return; voluntary exiles from the dangerous place our homeland is always becoming.

Cracks becomes, for many reasons, an amulet for and against New York in particular and America in general.

It is dedicated to Jack Hirschman, my southern brother who initiated a correspondence that lasted its full and glorious epoch. We became transformed into bent, mythic, oldtime kabbalists. Rolls of revelation and commentary poured out of our caves like Niagara. Most of it was done by letters, yet every so often we'd visit each other and spend night into day turning reality into a midrashic webwork, a mystic companion shadowing us and our works, overseeing our energies with tolerance. Haunted by time—this time, that time— nagged and inspired by phantoms and golems and *gilgullim*, Jack embodies the drama of creation. Through speech we often emerged beyond language only to face the black doors of Hebrew alphabet whose ink we filled new visions with. Operas of talk and paper and *bet ha-midrash* love-labyrinth embrace of rare unique books. Jack's unerring 4th sense instinct for a book's secrets made going into second-hand bookshops an electrifying rite—the same applied to Jewish libraries we would enter like snipers, *Orphée* cartunes approaching each shelf with awe and high hopes, in quest of the book behind the book, the mystery inside the mystery.

Jack's generous and constantly available resources inspired the initial moment trance-forming me into an editor, a role wisely avoided up to that time. All of the issues of *Tree* are overtly or secretly dedicated to Jack Hirschman.

* * *

FILE-CARD NOTES
"crack(s)"—opening—into—out of—eye looking thru—

crack of lightning like tree rootsystem—central nervous system—
cracked—crazy—crack-up
crack—the opening of her sex
crack the nut's shell—Eleazer of Worms—"he who knows the science of the nut (*hakmoth ha-'egoz*) will know the depth (*'omeq*) of the Merkavah"—
wise-crack—Under Brooklyn light-post—Pitkin Avenue coin-flip artiste—
Joanne Kyger's "doo doo" poem—cracked head-glass —finally got thru—

"Oy
Oh great and gifted one thy devine
Thou Art
The gift from the singing trees trimmed in gold
Thou art the purple blossoms

Thou art the most superb motion

    Thou art into super doo doo fantasies
    recognizing the true worth of the word
    In All its cosmic flory and relief
    of nation to nation, minute to minute

Thou art never talking to thineself
Thou art the negative and positive
I mean that the negative is really positive, Thou Art.

    Thou Art Devine
    The True Doo Doo Fantasy of Heaven

    Thou Art Devine
    The True Doo Doo Fantasy of Heaven"

[from: *All This Every Day*. Big Sky, Bolinas, 1975.]

the fire cracking—

* * *

6] APPLE

As it stands. Part of the branch. Another attempt to personalize midrashic form, another commentary.

An exploration which first began with "A Mischnah Gas for SP, BZ:BD:BZ, JAH, AbA" which appeared in *Praxis: One*, edited by Stephen Pickering, scholar of Dylan Hermeneutics and *hasid;* its sequel was "From a Midrash" which appeared in *Tens: Selected Poems, 1961-1971;* the rest are in this book as you find them.

* * *

All translations.

* * *

My Kabbalah the English-American Kabbalah received via translation into language complexly reduced from Kabbalah's primary source: Hebrew. It was and is the poet's task to read between the silhouettes. To bring back or restore, most surely to continue.

To mis-quote Harold Bloom,[1] all of my work is a mis-reading of translations which themselves are mis-readings of a three-dimensional language existing to be read and mis-read until one comes to the end of the book, the beginning of the word.

* * *

---

1. *Kabbalah and Criticism* by Harold Bloom. Seabury Press, NY, 1975.

Printed August 1976 in Santa Barbara & Ann Arbor
for the Black Sparrow Press by Mackintosh & Young
and Edwards Brothers Inc. Design by Barbara Martin.
This edition is published in paper wrappers;
there are 200 copies numbered & signed by the
author; & 26 lettered copies handbound in boards
by Earle Gray each containing an original drawing
by David Meltzer.

Photo: Gerard Malanga

Autobiograph

At work on
1945, poem-prose sequence to that time—
Asaf, still in progress, five years old, large (massive) poem structure, Music as source of self-history—
collaborating with Allen Say on translations of stories by one of Japan's great writers, Shiga Naoya (1883-1971) and a collection of *rakugo*, elaborately funny stories from the Edo district, Tokugawa period—
still editing *Tree* (and Tree Books), a bi-annual journal devoted to exploring themes in Jewish mysticism—
just concluding a year-term, first time, teaching high-school at the Urban School, San Francisco—teaching poetry, jazz history, dreams and humour—
yet despite all this activity which is not as impressive as it might sound or look
I prefer to sit in the backyard garden watching whatever happens happen—in fact, I take sitting-in-the-garden to be the most impressive thing I do.

PS
3563
.E45
S5

PS
3563
.E45
S5

$4.00